The Reasons Why...

The Reasons Why...

The Reasons Why...

The Reasons Why...

www.writeous.org

The Reasons Why...

The Reasons Why...

www.writeous.org

The Reasons Why...

The Reasons Why...

The Reasons Why...

The Reasons Why...

The Reasons Why...

The Reasons Why...

The Reasons Why...

The Reasons Why...

The Reasons Why...

The Reasons Why...

The Reasons Why...

The Reasons Why...

The Reasons Why...

The Reasons Why...

The Reasons Why...

The Reasons Why...

The Reasons Why...

The Reasons Why...

The Reasons Why...

The Reasons Why...

The Reasons Why…

The Reasons Why...

The Reasons Why...

The Reasons Why...

The Reasons Why...

The Reasons Why...

The Reasons Why...

The Reasons Why...

www.writeous.org

The Reasons Why...

The Reasons Why...

The Reasons Why...

The Reasons Why...

The Reasons Why...

The Reasons Why...

The Reasons Why...

The Reasons Why...

The Reasons Why...

The Reasons Why...

The Reasons Why...

The Reasons Why...

The Reasons Why...

The Reasons Why...

The Reasons Why...

The Reasons Why...

The Reasons Why...

The Reasons Why...

The Reasons Why...

The Reasons Why...

The Reasons Why...

The Reasons Why...

The Reasons Why...

The Reasons Why...

The Reasons Why...

The Reasons Why...

The Reasons Why...

The Reasons Why...

www.writeous.org

The Reasons Why...

The Reasons Why...

The Reasons Why...

The Reasons Why...

The Reasons Why...

The Reasons Why...

The Reasons Why...

The Reasons Why...

www.writeous.org

The Reasons Why...

The Reasons Why...

The Reasons Why...

The Reasons Why...

The Reasons Why...

The Reasons Why...

The Reasons Why...

The Reasons Why...

The Reasons Why...

The Reasons Why...

The Reasons Why...

The Reasons Why...

The Reasons Why...

The Reasons Why...

The Reasons Why...

The Reasons Why...

The Reasons Why...

The Reasons Why...

The Reasons Why...

The Reasons Why...

The Reasons Why...

The Reasons Why...

The Reasons Why...

The Reasons Why...

The Reasons Why...

The Reasons Why...

The Reasons Why...

The Reasons Why...

The Reasons Why...

PLEASE

FOR
GIVE
ME

THE END

Made in the USA
Monee, IL
04 November 2026

67379710R00056